P9-ELX-613

DATE DUE

The Library Store #47-0152

AVON PUBLIC LIBRARY
BOX 977 / 200 BENCHMARK RD.
AVON, COLORADO 81620

Country Living
AMERICAN
Style
DECORATE ★ CREATE ★ CELEBRATE

HEARST BOOKS

New York

HEARST BOOKS
New York

An Imprint of Sterling Publishing
1166 Avenue of the Americas
New York, NY 10036

Country Living is a registered trademark of Hearst Communications, Inc.

© 2015 by Hearst Communications, Inc.

All rights reserved. No part of this publication may be reproduced, stored in
a retrieval system, or transmitted in any form or by any means (including electronic,
mechanical, photocopying, recording, or otherwise) without prior written
permission from the publisher.

Every effort has been made to ensure that all the information in this book
is accurate. However, due to differing conditions, tools, and individual skills,
the publisher cannot be responsible for any injuries, losses, and/or other damages
that may result from the use of the information in this book.

ISBN 978-1-61837-129-4

BOOK DESIGN BY ANNA CHRISTIAN

Distributed in Canada by Sterling Publishing
c/o Canadian Manda Group, 664 Annette Street
Toronto, Ontario, Canada M6S 2C8
Distributed in Australia by Capricorn Link (Australia) Pty. Ltd.
P.O. Box 704, Windsor, NSW 2756, Australia

For information about custom editions, special sales, and premium
and corporate purchases, please contact Sterling Special Sales
at 800-805-5489 or specialsales@sterlingpublishing.com.

Manufactured in China

2 4 6 8 10 9 7 5 3 1

www.sterlingpublishing.com

CONTENTS

WELCOME!

One of the best things about working at a magazine that celebrates the country lifestyle is the ability to peek into homes all across the nation and discover a whole world of ideas under each roof: from Arkansas to Oregon, Maine, Texas, and everywhere in between. Each state and region has its own flavor and traditions, of course—a cabin in Montana has a different twist from one in North Carolina. I'm continually amazed and inspired by the resourceful, clever, creative, and welcoming ways Americans make their homes their own.

In this book, we shine a light on the many reasons American style is so special and showcase products that are proudly made in America, by Americans, including gorgeous wallpapers, bakeware, china, furniture, and flags. We feel lucky to have such a diverse bounty to draw from, champion, and admire.

—Rachel Hardage Barrett, *Editor-in-Chief*

What is AMERICAN STYLE?

How our nation's history and character are reflected as elements in the design of our homes

You could say that the American Revolution is the best explanation for the evolution of American design. As a scrappy, ragtag band of colonists, we had the hubris to challenge old-guard England, with its formal class system and associated trappings: high teas, kings, and queens. Here in the States, a country founded just over 200 years ago, we don't have ruins or medieval relics to riff on or emulate. What we do possess are the values of our founding mothers and fathers: thrift, ingenuity, and daring. We value the striking simplicity of the handmade wooden furniture developed by our Shaker ancestors, not to mention colorful Navajo blankets and the intricacy of Nantucket baskets. Plus, we give ourselves the freedom to mix things up. We celebrate bold, spirited choices, and the way we entertain is wonderfully informal. We eat in the kitchen or on the porch and host come-one, come-all barbecues. We take pride in handmade and American-made goods, practical solutions, finding new uses for old things, items that show off our individuality—and breaking more rules than we follow. We think Thomas Jefferson—who believed there ought to be a revolution every 20 years—would approve.

◄ **Cast in rich reds and oranges,** classic wool trading blankets convey warmth—in every sense of the word.

two

WAYS TO

celebrate your American history

◄◄ **By showing where you come from . . .** A circa 1900 map of New Hampshire hangs alongside the homeowner's paintings of her grandsons, telling the story of their family ties and state pride. The map itself is imbued with all kinds of meaning: The homeowners got engaged hiking one of those steep White Mountain trails.

◄ **. . . or honoring the people who made you who you are.** Pay homage to your family's unique history with these instant-heirloom embroidery hoop frames. Held in place with hand-embroidered "photo corners," black and white snapshots take on a polished presence. (This crafty solution also gets your treasures out in the open where you can appreciate them, instead of letting them languish squirreled away in albums or desk drawers.)

◄◄ Primitive turns chic.
Take another look at milking stools and quilts. These beauties prove that a coat of milk paint, or an aerial satellite map rendered in salvaged plaid shirts and silk, take oldies-but-goodies to a wonderfully artistic and unexpected new place.

◄ Go on a cross-country tour—without leaving your chair. You can take in our nation's most breathtaking sights with digital prints (*printcollection.com*) of 1930s-era travel posters commissioned by the WPA—the agency that put unemployed artists to work.

PORTRAIT
OF AMERICA

YORK WALLCOVERINGS
York, Pennsylvania

York wallpaper has been printed in the same Pennsylvania factory for 117 years.

Before the Industrial Revolution, wallpaper often cost big bucks. But mid-19th-century innovations (including the advent of the roller press) lowered prices, and middle-class Americans went mad for the home-decorating material—even redoing rooms seasonally. In 1895, six York, Pennsylvania, businessmen decided to cash in on the trend by establishing the York Wall Paper Co. Today, the enterprise is still going strong in its original headquarters, producing more than 100 million feet of wallpaper a year.

1935 ⇒ Sears, Roebuck & Co. offers York wares through its mail-order catalog.

1945 ⇒ After World War II, the U.S. government lifts a restriction forbidding new wallpaper designs. Three years later, York launches the White Rose floral collection with the brand's first major ad campaign, seen in *House Beautiful* and other magazines.

1986 ⇒ The Reagans decorate Camp David with a hunting scene by the company, now called York Wallcoverings.

2002 ⇒ York debuts a line of easy-to-remove wallpaper aimed at apartment dwellers.

2010 ⇒ The Academy Award–nominated movie *Black Swan* features a York butterfly motif in the bedroom of Natalie Portman's ballerina character.

▶ Talk about a winning color palette
Playing with patterns in iconic shades of red, white, and blue offers a spirited spin on classic country. Items imbued with their own history—like a vintage quilt or flag-inspired throw pillow—strengthen the patriotic effect.

two

WAYS TO

say relax!

▲ **By choosing indoor/ outdoor furniture ...** There was a time when folks protected their living room furniture with do-not-touch plastic covers. Blessedly, that time has passed, and living rooms, especially, have really loosened up. This rattan-based sectional and cheerful ticking–stripe rug invite rowdy games of checkers and lazy afternoons.

▶ **... or by piling on the pillows** This built-in daybed in Massachusetts gets its plush, inviting character not from fancy shams, but from a mass of throw pillows covered in an assortment of blue and white napkins.

▲ **Step away from the silver polish!** Nine times out of ten, an easy, aw-shucks informality—like pressing a potting bench into service as a sideboard decked out with lemonade and wildflowers—is the secret to putting guests at ease.

◄ **Radiate a put-your-feet-up warmth.** Even on the coldest days of winter, this New Hampshire living room glows thanks to casually propped paintings, mini pumpkins, armfuls of bittersweet berries, and, of course, a roaring fire.

▲ **A stack of vintage valises adds up to one stunning side table.** Bonus: These suitcases also provide first-class storage for off-season clothes.

▶ **A pair of apple crates finds new life as a charmingly wholesome bedside stand.** Shed even more light on this clever concept by using a drill and a pendant lamp kit from the hardware store to turn Mason jars into lamps.

LODGE MANUFACTURING
South Pittsburg, Tennessee

With a 116-year history, Tennessee's Lodge skillets are no flash in the pan.

Some folks might have just given up. But when a 1910 fire destroyed Joseph Lodge's 14-year-old Blacklock Foundry in South Pittsburg, Tennessee, the businessman rebuilt his company in a matter of months—this time, giving it his own name. More than a century later, Lodge Manufacturing's skillets remain the cookware of choice for discriminating chefs: Both John Currence and Alton Brown swear by the pans—and the ones shown here cost just $6.95 to $36.95!

1965 ➤➤ Lodge modernizes its molding process, switching from hand-pouring to automated machinery.

1980s ➤➤ Demand for the brand's skillets soars as home cooks attempt New Orleans chef Paul Prudhomme's wildly popular blackened redfish.

2002 ➤➤ The firm debuts the very first pre-seasoned cast-iron cookware.

2012 ➤➤ Run by the founder's great-grandchildren, Lodge crafts up to 1,600 pieces an hour at its factory on the banks of the Tennessee River.

PORTRAIT
OF AMERICA

◄ **The best flea marketers see things for what they could become.** To wit, these artful sconces trimmed with burlap fringe were fashioned from $10 cow-feed sifters. Likewise, the frame of the daybed is made from an old $25 door and wooden shipping pallets.

▶ **From trash to treasure** The moment she spotted this bedspring at an antiques shop, the owner of this Texas home envisioned it as a show-stopping memo board.

▲ **Make every space count.** This North Carolina house boasts a full-fledged office—on an otherwise wasted stair landing.

▲ **Celebrate homegrown ingenuity.** What's an inventive—and inexpensive— way to praise American innovations? By downloading images, like these vintage garden tools, from google.com/patents and having them printed onto large-scale paper at a copy shop for less than five bucks apiece.

▲ **Redefine the "formal" dining room.** Any area big enough for a table and chairs can host a proper sit-down—just check out this Ohio home's magnificent "hallway" for proof.

three

IDEAS FOR

dirt-cheap collections

◀ **Get hooked on colorful fishing flies . . .** It's no wonder they're irresistible; these beauties are designed to be eye-catching.

▲ **. . . maximize the charm of old watering cans . . .** This elevated assortment marries form and function.

▶ **. . . or fall for an assortment of (totally free) leaves.** Pressed foliage doesn't even require frames: Each leaf is simply adhered to card stock with spray mount.

two

WAYS TO

create
high-impact
tableaux

▼ **Cluster like objects together . . .** Rather than reading as clutter, repetition creates a polished scene. Just look at the statement-making possibilities of yellow pottery.

▶ **. . . or dedicate a display case to your finds.** Arranged with room to breathe in its own cabinet, humble white hobnail takes a picture-perfect turn.

HOMER LAUGHLIN CHINA CO.

Newell, West Virginia

Fiesta ware—produced by West Virginia's Homer Laughlin China—has been cheering up tables since 1936.

As American mealtimes grew more casual in the 1930s—with families eating in the kitchen—Homer Laughlin China Co. responded by introducing a line of informal dinnerware called Fiesta. Designed by Frederick Hurten Rhead, art director of the Newell, West Virginia, outfit, the dishes sported a handcrafted look in bright colors such as red, blue, and green. Here's how the goods became collector's items:

1936 ➤➤ Just six months into production, the factory turns out its millionth piece of Fiesta.

1950 ➤➤ Hues shift with trends, and pastels emerge; 10 years later, a bolder palette returns.

1973 ➤➤ Believing the style had run its course, Homer Laughlin discontinues the line.

1986 ➤➤ Demand for vintage Fiesta leads to a relaunch.

1988 ➤➤ Andy Warhol's 332-item assortment of Fiesta ware brings $11,550 at auction.

2008 ➤➤ *The Mentalist* joins a long list of TV shows and movies, including *Two and a Half Men* and *A Christmas Story*, to use the vibrant ceramics as props.

PORTRAIT
OF AMERICA

◄◄ **Check out the design-on-a-dime of this Montana cabin.** This "built-in" wall unit is really three $60 IKEA bookcases, tucked under the eaves and finished with trim. The 1950s Naugahyde club chair cost $5 at the Salvation Army. The vinyl plank flooring—at $3 per square foot—mimics the look of hardwood for a fraction of the cost. And the homeowner made over this thrift-store sleeper sofa by replacing the dated back cushions with Euro squares and sewing an all-white slipcover.

◄ **DIY and serendipity come together in this Oregon home.** The homeowner snapped the cattle photo with her phone, printed it at Costco for six bucks, and popped it in a $20 Michaels frame. A mail-room filing cabinet, scored for under $200 at a vintage shop, strikes an industrial note in the mudroom. And no one bid on this early-1900s birdcage at an area auction, so the homeowner nabbed it afterward for free.

◄ **Nothing beats the determination and resourcefulness of a budget-minded new bride.** At this former bachelor pad in North Carolina, the bride sewed the living room curtains herself, using sheer $9-a-yard fabric from Grayline linen. The handsome $250 1920s cane sofa came from Craigslist. Three $12 hardware-store drop cloths made reupholstering the sofa and the wingback chair (a $20 Goodwill find) downright inexpensive. But the biggest coup might be the $60 wardrobe—fronted with two $20 custom-cut Lowe's mirrors—that hides the couple's TV.

Five
REASONS TO LOVE
FIXER-UPPERS

1 Americans adore a bargain.

2 Realizing the potential of a diamond in the rough is fulfilling work. Especially once it's over.

3 Old houses that need work often qualify for historic rehabilitation tax credits from the IRS. Ka-ching!

4 You won't have to pay for someone else's questionable or faddish "upgrades."

5 They just don't build 'em like they used to.

◀ **Look beyond the usual upholstery fabric sources.** Searching for ticking stripes on eBay yielded this fabric—for just $2 per yard.

▲ **Better yet, skip reupholstering altogether.** This slipcovered seat got a face-lift—fast—from a folded, lightweight cotton rug.

Practical Inspiration from COAST to COAST

**Whether rustic, refined, or in between,
the secrets to capturing our country's most beloved styles**

If you start to dissect enough photos of beautiful rooms, certain themes and tricks emerge. Some homeowners simply have an instinct for adding just the right amount of sparkle, or even a ruffle or two, to make a room feel stop-you-in-your-tracks pretty but not overly sweet. Others throw in an element of surprise to loosen up the formality of a room filled with handsome antiques.

Arriving at that balance is no easy feat. Don't have that instinct? Have no fear! In this chapter, we're going to decode and demystify the process, so you can master the right mix of tradition with a twist, rustic revival, or stunningly refined glamour in your home. Even a whole row of milking stools can look fresh if the surroundings are kept crisp and spare. Likewise, we show when to take risks with wild fabrics and how to incorporate bark-covered log and twig furniture in a contemporary way. They're not rules so much as shortcuts to arriving at a look that delights you—because in the end, that's truly all that matters.

◄ **The spareness of this California bedroom**—presided over by a flea-market oil portrait—makes the entire scene itself look like a masterful painting.

L.L.BEAN

Brunswick, Maine

Maine outfitter L.L.Bean still fashions every Boat and Tote at its Brunswick factory.

In 1944, 32 years after launching his mail-order business, Leon Leonwood Bean constructed a sturdy canvas sack for hauling the heavy frozen blocks used in iceboxes of the day. Over the past six decades, this utilitarian accessory has evolved into an icon of effortless, all-American style (Reese Witherspoon and Julia Roberts are fans). As a matter of fact, the company manufactures up to 2,500 of the bags daily in Brunswick, Maine.

1945 ➤➤ L.L. Bean nixes the carrier from his catalog.

1965 ➤➤ The founder's grandson Leon Gorman adds colored trim to the defunct design, reintroducing it as the Boat and Tote.

1980 ➤➤ Lisa Birnbach's *The Official Preppy Handbook* raves, "Bean is nothing less than Prep mecca," and sales of the Boat and Totes continue to soar.

1991 ➤➤ Personalize it! Bean starts monogramming the bags.

2005 ➤➤ Custom Boat and Totes debut: Shoppers can pick fabric hues, handle lengths, and more—bringing the possible variations to 400,000.

PORTRAIT OF AMERICA

◀ **Wit is essential.** A dash of humor keeps a formal interior from feeling stiff. In this hundred-year-old New York–state home, a cheeky pheasant topper, placed on the newel post, acts as a foil to the stately paneled woodwork, wall of landscapes, and woven runner.

▲ **Yes, you can paint wood.** Converting this 1920s Oregon barn to a winning guesthouse required camouflaging mismatched floors with porch paint in demure gray. "It's never my instinct to paint wood," the homeowner said, "but this saved us from having to tear out all the boards." Plus, the nearly all-white palette makes the antique-style hardware, brass candlesticks, and other old-school elements feel fresh.

two

WAYS TO

make the most of risk-taking fabrics

▲ **Pair them with traditional shapes.** In Europe, this hand-me-down daybed would be covered in pale silk or neutral linen, but in Vermont, bold ikat and apple green velvet demonstrate one homeowner's free-spirited vision to amazing effect.

▶ **Push the envelope with primary colors.** Bold tomato-colored upholstery—paired with yellow woodwork, no less—tricks the eye into seeing these two similarly shaped chairs as a matching pair.

◄ **Look up for inspiration.** Jaunty stripes strike an unexpectedly playful note in the Massachusetts bedroom of this historic lodge-turned-home.

▲ **Give gingham an edge.** To make a sweet-as-apple-pie interior really sing, bring in one curveball like the ultra-contemporary chairs in this Montana dining room.

▲ **The bigger the pattern, the greater the effect.** The super-sized scale of the wallpaper imbues this California bedroom with a luxe vacation-villa vibe.

▶ **Contrast = instant glamour.** In fashion designer Tracy Reese's country retreat, a sweet sundress, gauzy curtains, and white ceramics take on ten times the presence—in a delightfully girlish way—against the black walls of her bedroom.

▲ **Strike a coquettish note.** When glamour is the goal, a room needs a dash of Scarlett O'Hara.

▲ **Ruffle revival** Soft gathers also add a little something to shower curtains and towels.

◄ **Bring on the bling.** The feminine mystique of this 1900 Arkansas cottage comes from the sage cupboard, arched windows, pitcher of wildflowers, and the window seat dotted with rose-covered cushions, of course. But most of all, the room derives its sparkling flourish from the prisms dangling from the chandelier.

★★ *Five* ★★
REASONS TO LOVE
LOG CABINS

1 A tribute to early settlers and pioneers, the log cabin is one of the original American architectural styles

2 The historic ones are made from good old USA-grown timbers, like cypress and ponderosa pine

3 Hand-hewn and exposed beams allow the beauty of wood's grain to shine through.

4 Hearths and sleeping lofts, like the ones described by Laura Ingalls Wilder, make these homes undeniably cozy!

5 They're versatile! Some of the most famous examples—like Yellowstone National Park's Old Faithful Inn, with its eight-story lobby that is some 185 feet high—show off this rustic construction's gloriously grand side.

◄ Seek out intact wood in a variety of shapes and sizes. Furniture crafted from branches, logs, and twigs mingles with a retro sign, modernist lamps, and fanciful bedside tables to make rustic revival work in this Georgia home.

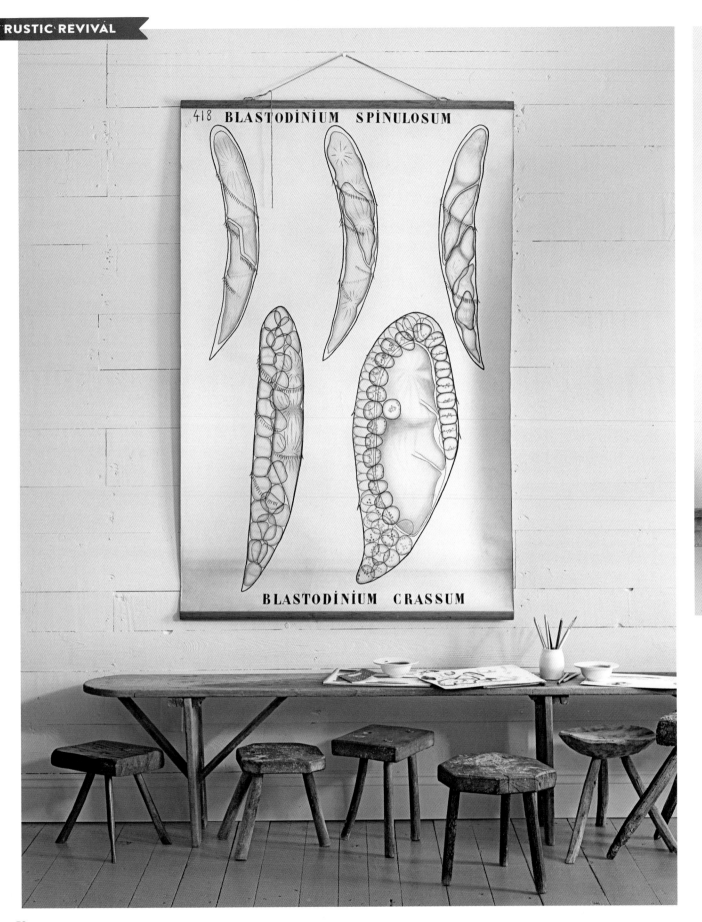

DELAWARE COUNTY FAIR

Walton, New York

The enduring tradition of the county fair keeps us connected to the farm life.

What ➟ Each summer in small towns across the nation, festivals like this one bring communities together to exhibit livestock, show off baking skills, and reconnect with America's agricultural roots.

When ➟ The Delaware County Fair, started in 1841, pays homage to tradition with classic events such as tractor pulls and vegetable contests.

Why ➟ It's the junior farm program's 4-H members—including Darby Reynolds (below) with her prize hog, Spot—who provide hope for the future.

(delawarecountyfair.org)

PORTRAIT OF AMERICA

◀ **Keep it spare.** Decor doesn't get more down home than an arrangement of milking benches and stools, but the minimalism of this tableau, accented with a vintage biology chart, makes sure any potential hokeyness stays far, far at bay.

▲ **Bring on the barnyard!** You simply can't achieve the warmth and charm of the new rusticity without a few roosters, pigs, sheep, or cows. Whether on china or as accessories, animal motifs serve as a reminder of our country's agricultural roots—while also being just plain adorable.

two

WAYS TO

incorporate sculptural elements

▶ **Seek out man-made tools that tell a story . . .** This primitive installation of wooden implements and a cow painting mounted on an old gate gets the gallery treatment in a New York–state farmhouse. Because the scene is stripped of tchotchkes and unnecessary elements, each rough-hewn element shines as art.

▶▶ **. . . or look for objects with all-natural appeal.** Both outdoorsy and chic, the beauty of this bench in Rhode Island comes entirely from the arcs and spikes of shed antlers.

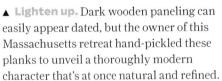

▲ **Lighten up.** Dark wooden paneling can easily appear dated, but the owner of this Massachusetts retreat hand-pickled these planks to unveil a thoroughly modern character that's at once natural and refined.

▶▶ **Transform the usual tropes.** Rescued from macho hunting and fishing clubs and recast in pure white, thanks to spray paint, this Montana cabin's collection of winter sporting goods reads as brilliant—and locally inspired—wall art.

IVERSON SNOWSHOES

Shingleton, Michigan

Iverson Snowshoes keeps traditional techniques alive in Michigan.

Back in 1956, Clarence Iverson transformed his Shingleton, Michigan, garage into a workshop, and soon local hunters and foresters were snapping up his bentwood and rawhide snowshoes.

1959 ➤➤ Iverson introduces moisture-resistant neoprene lacing as a low-maintenance alternative to the original varnished rawhide.

1971 ➤➤ L.L.Bean starts carrying the snowshoes, and continues to offer Iverson's best-selling Green Mountain design.

2010 ➤➤ Now owned by Shingleton natives Bob and Linda Graves, Iverson Snowshoes adds a high-performance racing model, constructed of white ash from Michigan's Upper Peninsula.

PORTRAIT OF AMERICA

All-American
FURNISHINGS

Pedestal tables, wing chairs, and other love-forever
favorites that never go out of fashion

Aside from museums and historic house tours at Colonial Williamsburg or Deerfield, you're unlikely to see strict "period" rooms in examples of stylish American decorating. What's far more interesting—as well as fun—is having the freedom to celebrate the dramatic tension between old and new, conservative and colorful, functional versus the occasional flight of fancy.

What's not fun is splurging on a big purchase you regret, and the pressure to choose wisely can be paralyzing. To pull its weight, a truly great chair should adapt seamlessly to your life. But what if you move from condo to country cottage? How can you be sure that sofa will be at home in your next living room?

Here's a secret to choosing furniture you'll love forever: The more expensive the purchase you're making, the more classic the design should be. Certain key pieces work in a pied-à-terre or a rambling ranch, and here we've highlighted some that will help you decorate without regret: a pair of upholstered armchairs to flank a fireplace or dining table; a bench to tuck at the end of a bed or under a staircase; a slim-lined pedestal table beside a sofa or in the guest room. These pieces work wherever you call home. Iconic shapes serve as anchors in any room so you can play with mood and personal style. Pillows, paint, lampshades, and linens can transform the feeling of a space as tastes and trends change. Your love of ikats and polka dots may come and go, but good bones are forever.

◄ **The owners of this lakeside home** in Georgia filled their
great room with pieces they'll never tire of.

▲ **A fresh way to mix and match.** In Pennsylvania, tradition proves its versatility when a Colonial-style wood four-poster is dressed with florals and ethnic-print pillows, and is perfectly at home atop a modern, geometric print rug.

◀ **Industrial materials meet feminine form.** A soaring wrought-iron princess bed amps up the glamour of this luxurious Georgia bedroom replete with a vintage Richard Avedon print, mirrored nightstands, and a faux-fur throw.

Five
★★ REASONS TO LOVE ★★
a statement-making
BED

1 A great bed does all the heavy lifting for you—form, function, and drama all in one, which means you're less reliant on art and other elements to make the room pop.

2 Unlike high heels, home style doesn't make you sacrifice style for comfort—the two go hand in hand here.

3 Add a vintage breakfast tray and it's the most comfortable snack spot in the house.

4 It's not just furniture—a stand-out bed is the centerpiece of a room of your own where you can read, daydream, and luxuriate in quiet.

5 Four-poster, canopy, wrought iron or wood, the frame you love stays the same but the linens you dress it with can transform the look and feel of an entire room.

▲ **The staying power of spindles** Perennially stylish since it first became popular in the 17th century, the spindle-style bed—piled with graphic, modern textiles in this Arkansas bedroom—stands out against rough-hewn walls.

▶ **Start strong.** The powerful symmetry of a traditional four-poster frame allows for more offbeat choices, like the mismatched bedside tables in this stylish bedroom.

◄ **Tailored and timeless**
Standing formally in front
of a wall of French doors, a
perfectly proper roll-over arm
sofa bridges the gap between
a dark, traditional pedestal
table and lamp, and a sleek
marble-topped coffee table in
this Washington, D.C., home.

▲ **Light and bright** An always-in-style white sofa requires only a row of playful pillows to create a room that's whimsical and fresh.

▶ **Neutral and stunning** The value of thrift is writ large in an understated California living room, where a swap-meet Chesterfield sofa is reupholstered with IKEA linen.

Five
★★ REASONS TO LOVE ★★
a
COMFY SOFA

1 You can take it with you. A classic silhouette will work in a farmhouse or a loft.

2 It's up for whatever challenge you throw its way—movie marathons, cocktail parties, card games, or just you, kicking your feet up after a long day.

3 You can go crazy with slipcovers or pillows, as sparkles, rainbows, and needlepoint motifs come and go, guilt-free.

4 It doesn't just work in the living room. Slide one at the foot of the bed or tuck it into a reading nook—or wherever you want a nice, soft landing.

5 Stiff settees might be pretty to look at, but you'll never regret choosing function over mere form. With a great couch, comfort is king.

◄ **Building a more versatile living room**
A simple box-pleat sofa pulled up to a 30-inch-tall
table creates a casual living room spot for family
dinners, homework sessions, and late-night
card games.

▲ **A library you'll want to live in** Luxe and
masculine, a blue leather Chesterfield brings
a bookish regality to this Ohio farmhouse.

★★ *Five* ★★
REASONS TO LOVE
a pair of
UPHOLSTERED CHAIRS

1 They're probably the most comfortable—and versatile—seating there is. This plush duo can flank a fireplace, bedroom window, or even a dining room table.

2 Mirror-image armchairs bring symmetry and order to any room they're in. (Or split up the pair and marvel at how well they stand up on their own.)

3 Small and unobtrusive, soft chairs can slide in anywhere you want comfort but can't squeeze a sofa.

4 Their classic forms are the perfect place to go wild with prints: ticking stripes, botanicals, or wash-off-whatever-happens white slipcovers.

5 Wherever you put them, armchairs bring an invitation to relax and reconnect—with a book, a friend, or the fire.

▲ **What chic farmhouse pattern mixing looks like.** Grain sacks and stripes combine to create a modern farmhouse vibe on these two perches by the fireplace.

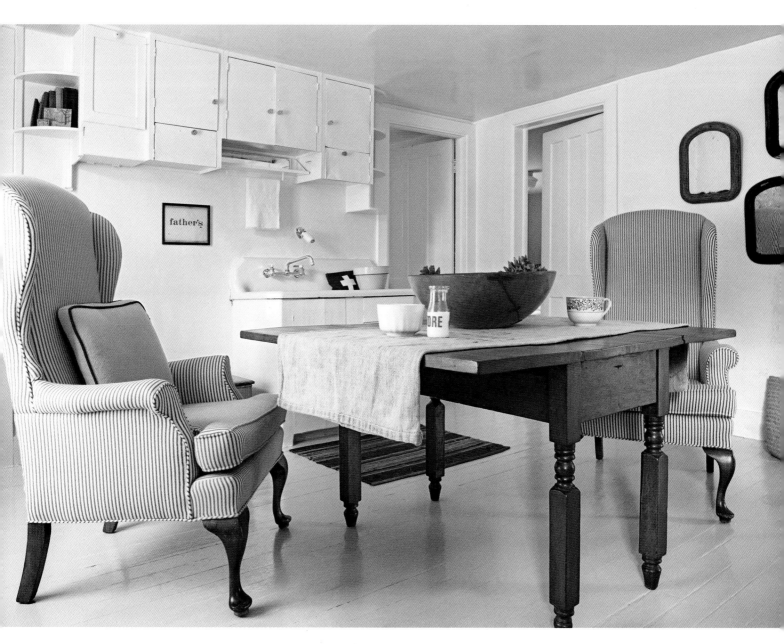

▲ **Make breakfast something worth lingering over.** These wing chairs bring living room luxury to this New York–state dining room.

▲ **Refined slipcovers (yes, there's such a thing)**
Curvy, white slipcovered armchairs can go anywhere,
but they're particularly fetching when festooned with floral
pillows as shown in this Mississippi living room.

◄ **Strong, silent types** Traditional ticking on
two inviting armchairs tempers more personality-
driven design choices, such as a vintage poster and
a 1960s resin elephant side table.

◄ How to mix and match old and new. Modern Windsor chairs and slat-back benches (all bargains from a big-box store) surround an oak tailor's table from the 1840s underneath hand-forged iron chandeliers in this Texas home.

▲ Classics can get modern renderings. Icons need not be staid, as these witty high-backed Windsors in a sunlight-soaked breakfast spot prove.

★★ *Five* ★★
REASONS TO LOVE
Windsor-style
CHAIRS

1 They might have originated in England, but Windsor chairs are thoroughly American: They were the seats of choice for our founding fathers in the Continental Congress.

2 A Windsor's spare, simple shape makes it a sculptural piece in a city condo or at a country farmhouse table.

3 They're affordable. Cheapo reproductions are—let's admit it—just as striking as the genuine article. (And they're easy to snatch up for a song in antique shops and flea markets, too.)

4 Placed next to a guest bed and topped with an alarm and an empty jam jar of garden blooms, these chairs do double duty as a cool, relaxed bedside tables.

5 More is more, and you can't have too many. Pull Windsor chairs up to the dining table or your desk; place one in the hallway or by the front door.

◄ **Perfectly patina-ed** Pulled up to a late-1800s farm table, reproduction Windsors hold their own in a Massachusetts dining room filled with historic Americana, like seascapes and soda bottles.

▼ **Pared down (and not at all pricey)** In this simple breakfast nook, a bright-red paint job and a streamlined silhouette recharge one of the most timeless designs in the decorating playbook—at a price ($35 at IKEA!) that'll sit well with your wallet.

THOS. MOSER CABINETMAKERS

Auburn, Maine

Maine's Thomas Moser builds on four decades of furniture craftsmanship.

Communications professor Thomas Moser fashioned clean-lined pine chairs and tables in his home workshop for 14 years before turning his hobby into a career in 1972. Since then, Thos. Moser Cabinetmakers, the Auburn, Maine, company he founded with his wife, Mary, has gone on to open showrooms across the country—and bring in millions in sales each year.

1973 ⇒ After placing an ad in Maine's *Down East* magazine, Moser sells his first piece, an occasional stand, for $140. The same model now retails for roughly $900.

1977 ⇒ The Windsor-esque continuous armchair debuts—and goes on to become the brand's top seller.

1991 ⇒ Thos. Moser crafts gallery benches for the Reagan Presidential Library in Simi Valley, California.

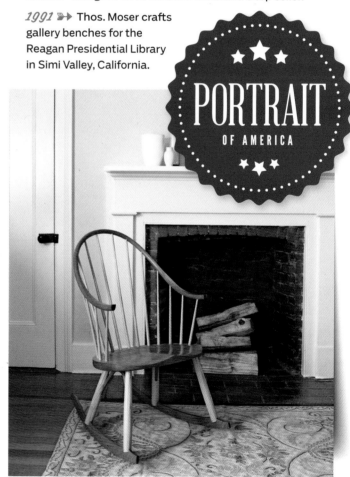

PORTRAIT OF AMERICA

◄ **Chairs can be local and organic, too.** In Vermont, natural elements like rough wood and ceramics adorned with flora and fauna organically share space with Windsor chairs and a farm table handmade by local Amish craftsmen.

▲ **The plant stand gets fancy.**
Topped with a lush fern, a tall pedestal
table transforms this Oregon bathroom
into a decidedly refined retreat.

▲ **Mid-century stunner** This beloved shape, designed by Finnish-American architect Eero Saarinen, was released by Knoll in 1957 and displays treasures in the foyer of a New York–state farmhouse.

▲ **Elevate mealtime.** Super-sized and surrounded by a banquette, the dining table anchoring this airy dining nook in California puts dinner on a pedestal.

★★ *Five* ★★
REASONS TO LOVE
PEDESTAL TABLES

1 They're thoroughly American. Colonial candle stands were some of the first pedestal tables.

2 They grew to wide popularity in the Victorian era, and large oak dining table interpretations could be bought from the Sears catalog in the early 1900s for about $25.

3 Alongside a king-sized bed or slim, little slipper chair, these handy stands are the perfect perch for drinks or books.

4 They give your soft, leafy ferns and favorite *objets d'art* all the attention they deserve.

5 The oversized versions make stunning dining tables—without the usual jumble of table legs.

▶ **Placement is everything.** A leggy vintage art nouveau pedestal table finds its perfect home in the windowed turret of a Victorian San Francisco home.

Five ★★ REASONS TO LOVE ★★ *a versatile* BENCH

1 They work for you. Whether they're Shaker wood, or industrial metal, benches are all about streamlined functionality.

2 They can go low-key or totally luxe. In their most rustic forms, they bring a sense of the outdoors in. Plush and upholstered at the end of the bed, they turn a bedroom into a lady's boudoir.

3 Alongside a wall by the front door, a bench serves as an instant, one-piece landing strip— tote bag and groceries on top, shoes and sports equipment underneath.

4 Pulled alongside a dining table, benches create an instant, casual sense of community.

5 Their small footprint saves valuable floor space in the tightest of rooms.

▲ **Ready for a crowd**
In a breakfast nook, weathered oak benches provide ample seating at a vintage oak florist's table topped with zinc.

◄ **Always-right rattan** At this New Hampshire home, an inherited rattan piece placed at the foot of a bed and spruced up with new cushions became a perfect perch for slipping off shoes at the end of the day.

◄ **Take one last look.** Standing solidly against a vivid woodland wallpaper scene and underneath a convex mirror, a dresser in the hallway is the perfect place to check your lipstick or deposit your purse on your way in or out the door.

▼ **Old-fashioned flair**
Reproductions of 19th-century prints (a whaling scene and a diagram of weather vanes) hang above this Connecticut bedroom's simple, antique pine dresser.

Five
REASONS TO LOVE
a hold-everything
DRESSER

1 It can be pressed into service all throughout the house. In the bedroom, it's a handsome home for your clothes, but it can pinch-hit in the dining room as a sideboard stocked with linens, or it can store hats, gloves, and more in the foyer.

2 Drawers keep items tucked away and out of sight, but the top surface is an opportunity for display and decoration.

3 You can always have fun with hardware. Drawer pulls become an opportunity for artful, unexpected flair.

4 A mirror hovering over the top creates an instant—and infinitely more useful—take on the usual dressing table.

5 A coat of paint is all that's required to give a piece a whole new look.

The United States of COLOR

★ ★

How homeowners across the country are embracing the power of paint

Out of all the tools in a decorator's toolbox, good old-fashioned paint holds far and away the most magic. Nothing transforms a room faster (or cheaper) than color. It can perk up corners, hide flaws, amplify (or even create) a room's architecture, and utterly transform the look and feel of a space. The sky's the limit, and thankfully custom-mixed color comes at no extra cost. Sure, you can hire a pro to help out with the labor, but unlike wiring, plumbing, construction, or other heavy-duty jobs, you can also DIY—or call in a favor from kids or friends to get the job done in a snap.

We've gathered some of the most inspirational paint color moments to help you choose the ideal shades for your rooms with confidence. We'll arm you with unexpected ideas for blacks, browns, greens, and blues, along with sophisticated pinks, yellows, and stunning neutrals. We'll show you one-wall wonders, tricks for faking wallpaper, wainscoting, and more. And because a gorgeous high-gloss finish can be the knockout moment a room needs, and the old rule "flat finish for walls and satin for trim" no longer applies, we've included a primer to help you brush up on the all-new—and brilliant—basics.

◄ **Wring drama from an often overlooked spot,** like the humble stair risers in this New Hampshire home, with a spectrum of winning shades.

Where to Find Historical Paint Colors

★ Backed by solid research, these companies all offer period-appropriate hues:

★ Benjamin Moore's "Williamsburg" collection

★ The Old Fashioned Milk Paint Company

★ Olde Century Colors

▲ **Turn a liability into a stunning asset.** Vivid blue takes an oddly shaped attic wall from awkward to amazing in a New York seaside cottage.

▶ **Brighten your bookshelves.** This California home proves that you can have crisp white walls and color, too, with bookcases backed in bright blue.

★★ *Five* ★★
REASONS TO LOVE
a white
PICKET FENCE

1 This quintessentially American detail gives any residence a sense of wholesome nostalgia—no matter when it was built.

2 Picket fences also up the curb-appeal quotient of a home: The tidy painted perimeters offer a picture-perfect finishing touch.

3 They're functional and decorative, effectively corralling kids and animals without blocking attractive views.

4 In the colonial era, they were used to show property boundaries—now they're a favorite of landscape architects for edging garden beds.

5 They've captured the American dream in everything from *Modern Family* to *Father Knows Best*.

◀ **Frame your view.** Draw attention to the world beyond your windows by painting their sashes and mullions a striking yellow as in this New Hampshire house.

two
WAYS TO
temper
a sweet shade

▶ **. . . with a riot of pattern . . .**
In Tennessee, splashy toiles,
geometrics, and stripes throw
cool lavender a red-hot curve.

▶▶ **. . . or with accents of
acidic green.** While in Kansas,
a handful of accessories—an
ottoman made edgy with sharp
lime upholstery, a cheeky bar,
and lots of bright foliage—
balance out this pretty pastel.

SQUARE BOOKS

Oxford, Mississippi

Across the nation, independent bookstores champion regional writers, host community gatherings, and keep the promise of the printed word going strong.

What ➤➤ Square Books is the heart of this small college town with a rich literary history: William Faulkner, Larry Brown, Barry Hannah, and Willie Morris all called Oxford home. Their work—and that of other Southern writers—is a focus for the store.

When ➤➤ Longtime resident and former mayor Richard Howorth opened the shop on the main square in 1979, explaining, "When I was growing up, there wasn't even a bookstore in Oxford."

Why ➤➤ "Unlike chain stores, nobody tells us what to buy," he says. "We order the books we think our customers will enjoy most."

◄ **Disguise dated brick.** A refreshing aqua helps a formerly ruddy fireplace in North Carolina blend in with the surrounding walls. (And an array of books fills the void of a non-working hearth with cheery color.)

▲ **Call on Mother Nature.** For a no-fail palette, pull your colors—sand, surf, sea glass—from the view outside, just like this Massachusetts escape.

▶ **Wake up a windowless bedroom.** In this Oregon home, low natural light is no problem when walls wear a perpetual peachy glow.

TABLES AND CHAIRS
CAN MAKE ROOMS POP

◄ **Pull a bolder shade from an existing palette . . .** Teal chairs only amplify the fresh effect of a cool aqua New York–state room.

▲ **. . . or go for all-out contrast.** In Kansas, a marigold pedestal table offers a stunning counterpart to a quiet, velvety brown wall color.

two

WAYS TO

cheer up
a tight spot

▶ **Hello, yellow!** Start your morning off right by recasting a cozy breakfast corner in a sunny shade, such as in this California bungalow.

▶▶ **Bring on the shine.** A lacquered finish ensures this enclosed bed in Oregon feels cozy and glamorous—not dim and cave-like.

LOUISVILLE STONEWARE

Louisville, Kentucky

Nearly two centuries of history shape Kentucky's Louisville Stoneware.

In 1815, entrepreneur Jacob Lewis opened Louisville, Kentucky's first ceramics workshop with a lofty goal in mind: proving that our then-fledgling nation could turn out pottery as fine as any made in England. His venture eventually went bankrupt, but Lewis left behind kilns, techniques, and designs that gave rise to the brand now known as Louisville Stoneware. And while the company has changed hands—and names—over the years, its artisans still carry on Lewis's tradition of craftsmanship, molding up to 120 tons of clay into dishes, garden accessories, and more each year.

1920–33 ➤➤ During Prohibition, the studio sees a spike in sales of jugs, shipping about three truckloads of moonshine holders to Chicago daily.

1938 ➤➤ The business branches out from no-frills salt-glazed crockery with the debut of brightly colored dinner sets.

1971 ➤➤ Louisville Stoneware introduces Bachelor Button, a floral motif created by in-house artist Edith Ellis; 40 years later, the pattern remains a favorite.

1985 ➤➤ To honor President Ronald Reagan, a fan of jelly beans, the brand fashions a candy dish in the shape of the White House for the commander-in-chief.

2011 ➤➤ Louisville Stoneware marks four decades as the official maker of earthenware mint-julep cups for Churchill Downs, home of the Kentucky Derby.

PORTRAIT OF AMERICA

◄ **Make an entrance.** Greet guests with a foyer painted with an inviting, rustic red. Hooks crafted from branches—cut down the middle and nailed to the wall— only add to the warm, down-home effect.

The New Rules PAINTING

Then ➤➤ Tacking up paint chips and hoping for the best.

Now ➤➤ Testing an eight-ounce sample pot on a piece of foam core that you can move and study in changing light.

Then ➤➤ Flat finish for walls; semi-gloss for kitchens, baths, and trim.

Now ➤➤ Yes, shine will show any imperfections—but if your walls are in good shape, go as glossy as you like.

Then ➤➤ Having to apply a separate coat of primer *every single time.*

Now ➤➤ Hallelujah! Top-tier formulas have primer built in, so only cases like stained or patterned surfaces require base layers.

◄◄ **Live large—even under the eaves.** Defying conventional wisdom by painting the walls and ceiling in one color as shown in this North Carolina bedroom functions like a black dress. It lengthens the lines of the sloped ceilings rather than chopping the room up, which is the decor equivalent of a white shirt paired with black pants.

◄ **Turn tradition on its head.** Trade customary white wainscoting for a bluish-green to send ceilings soaring.

TAKE ANOTHER LOOK AT ANYTHING-BUT-BASIC BLACK

▲ **Throw classic a curve.** Making the walls and trim of this Texas living room a high-gloss ebony throws the pale 1950s furniture into sharp relief.

▲ **Tiny spaces demand big gestures.**
Forget what you've heard about cramped quarters requiring light colors. Bold black lends great presence to this petite Pennsylvania bathroom.

▲ **Redefine your cocoon.** Create a retreat designed for a deep sleep, like this New York–state farmhouse, with bedroom walls the color of a nighttime sky.

◄ **Make wild work.** A grounding gray balances out a carnival of patterns and colors, such as the chair fabric, pendant lights, and framed wallpaper of this California home.

KICK YOUR KITCHEN UP A NOTCH

◄ **Help open storage shine.** In Texas, this fresh, mineral green elevates ordinary storage into a show-stopping focal point.

▶ **Go for broke.** Bathe everything—walls, cabinets, and trim—in high-gloss teal to turn a pint-sized kitchen into a gleaming jewel box, like this New York–state getaway.

▼ **Create a sense of calm.** A pale, dreamy, hue strikes a perpetually pretty—and peaceful—note in Connecticut in a room that tends to attract mess and chaos.

CLEVER IDEAS FOR CHALKBOARD PAINT

◀ **Make a magical mural.**
This moisture-friendly graphic is a feat of trompe l'oeil, with "bead board" on the bottom and "wallpaper" on top—rendered completely in chalk.

▶ **Strike a playful note.**
The usual tile is no match for a witty and ever-evolving blackboard backsplash.

Creative Alternatives to Wallpaper

Simple wheat paste turns these abundant materials into striking wall coverings, for less:

★ Newsprint

★ Novel pages

★ Oversized maps

three
WAYS TO
fake wallpaper

◀ **Upgrade your roller.**
Believe it or not, this woodland design is the work of paint, not paper, fashioned with a patterned rubber roller.

▲ **Simply cut and paste.**
These floral flourishes are paper cutouts adhered directly onto the walls.

▶ **Pick a high-contrast color.**
Try painting one fearless shade atop another—like this orange leaf design on a magenta wall. Don't want to freehand it? Shop for stencils at etsy.com.

DON'T OVERLOOK THE FLOOR!

▲ Add a dose of delight with pale,
variegated stripes . . .

▲ . . . extra wide preppy stripes . . .   ▲ . . . or a solid sea of blue.

three

WAYS TO

turn trash into treasure

◄◄ **Unify an assortment of castoffs.** Turn mismatched flea market finds—like this mirror and set of drawers—into a perfect pair with color.

◄ **Dress up a dingy dresser.** Bring architectural character to a chest of drawers in a weekend with glued-on fretwork covered with a unifying coat of creamy chalk paint.

► **Disguise drab office gear.** Spray-painted yellow and topped with plywood, three Goodwill filing cabinets—bought for $25 total—morphed into a handsome storage unit.

New-World TEXTURES and TEXTILES

Bead board, vintage blankets, and other high-impact surfaces that say, "Please touch"—and make an American house a home

Forget mere shape and size: The texture of our surroundings impacts our spaces in subtle—but sometimes bold and dramatic— ways. The careful placement of pillows in plush velvet and chenille can turn a stark sofa into an inviting nest. American style has evolved to mean artfully juxtaposed contrasting textures within the same space. Even more striking is our ability to create a mélange from the most humble elements of our agrarian heritage—chicken wire, barn board, enamelware, and Depression-glass— with sophisticated and modern statement pieces like leather loveseats, crystal chandeliers, and hand-knotted rugs.

Today, we relish the process of reclaiming items that show the patina of our past. At times we bring the forest to the table in the form of well-grained wood, arboreal embroidery, and stoneware. We bring the beach to the bedroom with thick, braided rope and fibers like sisal and jute. We bring the factory to the foyer with cast iron and stainless steel. All these textured elements add depth and interest to welcoming interiors.

◄ **A combination of nubby,** homespun fabric makes this bed inviting. Above, the gleam of a leather-trimmed mirror strikes a contrasting note.

RECONSIDER CHICKEN WIRE (REALLY!)

▶ **A modern "coop"** Rustic chicken wire brings subtle pattern and a down-home texture to cabinets topped with contemporary ceramics.

▼ **Do a double take.** Chicken wire also creates a dynamic juxtaposition with midcentury wire chairs in this North Carolina dining room.

★★★
PORTRAIT
OF AMERICA

KASPAR WIRE WORKS

Shiner, Texas

Texas-based Kaspar Wire Works marks over 100 years of industrial-chic products.

Once barbed wire debuted in the 1800s, most ranchers threw out their old metal fencing. But Shiner, Texas, farmer August Kaspar saw a business opportunity in all that scrap, turning it into baskets that he sold to neighbors for $1 each. More than a century later, his Kaspar Wire Works has grown into a $45-million-a-year brand.

1904 ⧽⧽ Kaspar quits growing crops to distribute his containers through local general stores.

1922 ⧽⧽ The company finds a new use for its goods: clothes-check bins at school gyms and pools.

1943–5 ⧽⧽ During World War II, the Navy buys 9,615 of the line's deep-fryer baskets.

1956 ⧽⧽ Kaspar Wire Works launches coin-operated newspaper racks; 55 years later, the *New York Times* and some 5,000 other periodicals employ the manufacturer's holders.

2006 ⧽⧽ The firm develops food storage for NASA shuttles.

2006 ⧽⧽ Kaspar's great-grandsons run the business.

◄◄ Help appliances shine. This stainless steel refrigerator does double duty as a design element, providing a reflective swath of visual interest against the deep gray shelving and woven willow storage basket.

◄ Every room needs something luminous. Metals come in more shapes and sizes—and finishes— than we can count. This room melds a galvanized aluminum box with a mottled finish, shiny brass candlesticks, and a tarnished server so that natural light can glint and glimmer across the mantel.

PORTRAIT OF AMERICA

L.E. SMITH GLASS

Mount Pleasant, Pennsylvania

Pennsylvania's L.E. Smith glass brings a colorful history to the table.

Louis E. Smith founded L.E. Smith Glass in 1907 for the sole purpose of making jars to hold the homemade mustard he peddled in Pennsylvania. By the time he left in 1911, the brand had grown to include 100-plus different items, among them dishes, cups, and pitchers. Here's what happened next:

1917 ⟫ The company starts producing headlight lenses for Ford Motors. Chevy, Buick, and Dodge deals follow.

1922 ⟫ A decade after discontinuing black glass—which it invented in 1925—L.E. Smith reintroduces the Depression-era hue for candlesticks, plates, and more.

2000 ⟫ Martha Stewart raves about an L.E. Smith dish on the *Late Show with David Letterman*, triggering a retail expansion from small shops to nationwide chains, including Williams-Sonoma. Annual sales skyrocket to $15 million.

2010 ⟫ L.E. Smith ships up to 5,000 pieces of tableware a week (in 30 colors!) from its Mount Pleasant, Pennsylvania, factory. The best-selling pattern? Hobnail.

▶ New life for old plaster

Deconstructing can be a decorating tool on its own, particularly in structures that feature traditional building materials. In this Georgia loft, a flat wall comes to life when layers of paint and paper are removed, leaving mottled plaster in pale neutral tones. A collection of shells, nests, antlers, and feathers only heightens the effect.

▲ **Rope shows its modern side.** Who says armchairs need to be upholstered in typical fabrics? A knotted twine cover lends some added geometry to this structured chair. A spool table with a coil of simple two-strand twisted rope creates a complementary geometric design.

▶ **Lighten the load with straw accessories.** At this New York beach cottage, the shingled porch—outfitted with a winning display of woven straw hats and bags—offers one last stop before beginning an adventure or finally landing at home.

PAUL'S HAT WORKS
San Francisco, California

Thanks to four women, this nearly century-old California hat shop is still tops.

What ⇥ Fedoras, bowlers, porkpies—you can have just about any style lid custom-made at this gem of a boutique, which has been on the same city block since 1918.

Who ⇥ Friends Abbie Dwelle, Kirsten Hove, Olivia Griffin, and Wendy Hawkins (pictured from left to right) had long been charmed by this neighborhood institution. So when the gals learned in 2009 that owner Michael Harris planned to close the store, they pooled their resources and bought the place. Harris repaid the favor by mentoring the budding artisans for six months before passing the torch.

Why ⇥ "Hats are still functional and fashionable," says Griffin. "People are once again caring how and where products are made, which works in our favor." (hatworksbypaul.com)

PORTRAIT
OF AMERICA

◄ **Chippy paint is a good thing.** Pair the flaked finish of weathered wood with the pure, clean quality of solid marble to create a washroom like this one in California that feels like a calm refuge.

▲ **The whitest whites** Monochromatic design
works well when it incorporates a variety of
surfaces. In this Oregon living room, whites
in distressed oak, knobby rattan, and smooth,
cool alabaster and marble summon a look that's
naturally beautiful.

▶ **Mother Nature gets edgy.** Give a fallen branch new life as coasters with naturally scalloped bark trim.

▼ **Wall and floor treatments do a balancing act.** Here, a truly symmetrical surface—white and red, squares upon squares—complements the wonderfully irregular texture of the knotty wood.

◀ **Varied finishes make wood pieces stand out.** Wood floors, wood paneling, and wood furniture need their own personality to work well together. Mix a lightly stained floor with a heavily distressed item of furniture to help a piece like this farm table in Arkansas pop.

The New Rules DECORATING

Then ➤➤ Always having to select dark-colored upholstery to hide stains.

Now ➤➤ Washable, bleachable white denim slipcovers reign supreme! As counter-intuitive as it may be, the lightest fabric turns out to be the most pet- and family-friendly choice.

Then ➤➤ Hitting one furniture store for a matching five-piece bedroom "set."

Now ➤➤ It's all about the mix: a tufted velvet headboard paired with a shiny, streamlined bedside lamp.

Then ➤➤ Living room sofas and chairs were reserved for special occasions and company and—yes—sometimes even covered with plastic!

Now ➤➤ Living rooms are for living—watching movies, doing homework, and putting your feet up.

▲ **The many faces of classic shutters** Behold what $100 worth of salvaged shutters in various hues did for this Nevada dining room.

◄ **Dipping a toe into wall textures** Want to make your walls pop but not quite ready for graphic wallpapers? For instant—and inexpensive— character, consider classic bead board, which gives one-color walls definition, shadows, and sensory interest.

** *Five* **
REASONS TO LOVE
STONE HOUSES

1 Typically built from locally quarried rocks or fieldstones, they tie you—in a deep, geological way—to the community where you live.

2 These beauties last for centuries, in part because they're fireproof and impervious to termites and other pests. Plus, they won't rot or warp and don't require ongoing maintenance, like painting and other repairs.

3 Natural insulation! The sun slowly heats up rocks during the day, and warmth is released as the temperature falls throughout the evening.

4 Stone comes in myriad colors, from the pale Aquia Creek sandstone George Washington selected for the Capitol Building to the glowing pink granite of Martha Stewart's house on Mt. Desert Island in Maine.

5 They're at once millions of years old yet can be breathtakingly modern—just look at Frank Lloyd Wright's Falling Water in Pennsylvania for proof.

▲ **Home is where the hearth is.** Go back to basics by adding materials in their most elemental and original form: Large granite fieldstones are asymmetrically cemented together into this striking Massachusetts cabin's fireplace and hearth.

four

IDEAS FOR

salvaged sweaters

◀ **A cozy addition to a simple fixture** Textiles and fibers usually know their place in a room—as upholstery, window treatments, and at the table. Here, a pendant gets upgraded with a cable-knit cloak made from a vintage wool sweater.

▲ **Give scuffs the slip.** Function meets comfort with a warm take on painted stool legs. Lose the rubber feet and save your wood floors from scuffs with soft-yet-durable knitted "socks" for each leg of a rustic milking stool.

▲ **Throw pillows take a smart turn.** Borrowing patterns normally featured on preppy pullovers, these neutral-colored covers allow complex needlework and special stitching to take center stage.

▲ **A handsome sleeve for a vase.** Give indoor flora a homey, wintry touch by wrapping vessels in sweater sleeves secured with hot glue.

CENTRAL YARN SHOP

Portland, Maine

Since 1949, this notions and knitting shop has kept Maine residents in buttons, yarn, and more.

What ⇢ This downtown store is packed from floor to ceiling with more than 1,000 different kinds of buttons (both vintage and new), plus thread, ribbon, and yarn in every color of the rainbow. Beyond its impressive inventory, though, Central Yarn serves as a hangout where crafters can take classes or simply pass an hour knitting or sewing with friends.

Who ⇢ Rhona Vosmus (left) took over 20 years ago from her parents, who started the business in 1949.

Why ⇢ "Around here, people knit in the bathtub, at red lights, and before they go to bed at night," Vosmus explains. "If you're between 20 and 80 years old and you live in Maine, you either knit or ski when it gets cold. Or both."

PORTRAIT
OF AMERICA

◄ **Choosing materials? Stick to the rule of threes.**
Essential design substances like wood, stone, metal, glass, plastics, and textiles work well in threes. Choose wisely: here, the wood and metal pieces have each been blanched in creamy hues—the perfect counterpart to the chunky knit blanket, nubby chenille bedding, and embroidered throw.

two

WAYS TO

make homespun modern

▲ **Give new meaning to "blanket" chest.** Quilts aren't just for beds anymore. Hand-quilting floral textiles with long stitches of bright thread produces a puckered patchwork used here to upholster a once-plain dresser.

▶ **Nothing beats the softness of fabric that's been washed a million times.** This California bedroom combines a 19th-century log cabin quilt with pillow covers made from old, linen grain sacks—while maintaining a contemporary aesthetic.

◄ Create a deep sensory experience.
In Idaho, a sheepskin rug offers a soft landing after a pine-scented bubble bath. It also creates definition between the bathing and sleeping spaces.

Unexpected Uses for Vintage Blankets

Put these sturdy beauties to work as re-envisioned textiles:

★ As drawer liners and pillow covers

★ Attached to frame-stretchers and hung as art

★ Boiled and used as rugs or doormats

▲ A dining rug where any color is the perfect match Dining area rugs need to be inviting but durable. Even better if light spills or specks are camouflaged. This low-profile braided rag rug, featuring a wide spectrum of hues, is the perfect foundation for a country table.

▶ The beauty of a threadbare runner Everything changes, including the pile, weave, and shades of brilliant color in this antique entry runner. The more traffic this foyer sees, the more this piece says, "Welcome to the fray."

PENDLETON

Portland, Oregon

A brief history of Oregon's Pendleton blankets

In 1909, brothers Clarence, Roy, and Chauncey Bishop opened a wool factory in the town of Pendleton, Oregon, distinguishing themselves by creating intricately patterned blankets for local Native American tribes. Today, Pendleton—which has expanded to offer clothing, rugs, and bedding—stacks up as the country's largest manufacturer of wool blankets.

1909 ⇶ After studying the design preferences of area Native American tribes, Pendleton rolls out its debut Indian trading blanket, a jacquard weave.

1916 ⇶ The Bishop brothers partner with the National Park Service to produce the Glacier National Park blanket, the first in an ongoing series celebrating treasured American landscapes.

1924 ⇶ Pendleton expands into men's apparel with men's shirts. Three years later, the Bishops introduce the Chief Joseph blanket, a tribute to the Nez Perce tribe's leader. It remains the company's best seller today.

1941 ⇶ During World War II, Pendleton devotes all its manufacturing to making blankets that keep American troops warm overseas.

1960 ⇶ A California band dubs itself the Pendletones in honor of the brand. Though the group later changes its name—to the Beach Boys—the members wear Pendleton shirts on their first album cover.

PORTRAIT OF AMERICA

MAKE A BLANKET STATEMENT

▲ **Bring it to a boil.** Felting wool—by agitating it in hot water—tightens up the fibers to make even thicker and denser upholstery.

▶ **DIY drapes** In Michigan, iconic wool trading blankets take a turn as breathtaking—and insulating— window treatments.

CHAPTER SIX

Celebrating Our Country's FAVORITE HOLIDAYS

Creative ideas for memorable 4th of July, Halloween, Thanksgiving, and Christmas festivities—with heart

It's not the size of the wrapped and ribboned haul underneath the Christmas tree or getting right-angle cross-hatches on the 4th of July burgers that matters, this much we know. Still, when the holidays get into full swing, it's all too easy to lose sight of what it really means to create a day that's magical.

Traditions and memories aren't made from perfect days but from thoughtful ones. Making a holiday truly meaningful is as easy as putting your heart into it—taking the time to create a simple centerpiece or getting your hands dirty in the kitchen.

Which is not to say a shortcut is never in order. Eating semi-homemade ice cream sandwiches after a parade brings just as much delight as a treat made entirely from scratch does—and leave you with more time on your hands to enjoy the celebration yourself.

The best holidays are the ones where we create a warm and welcoming atmosphere for the people we're celebrating with. Guests might not remember exactly how many herbs you used in your stuffing, but they will be able to summon, weeks or even months later, just how nourished they felt at your table.

◄ **A jingle-bell wreath** and mercury-glass tree dress up this Connecticut mantel.

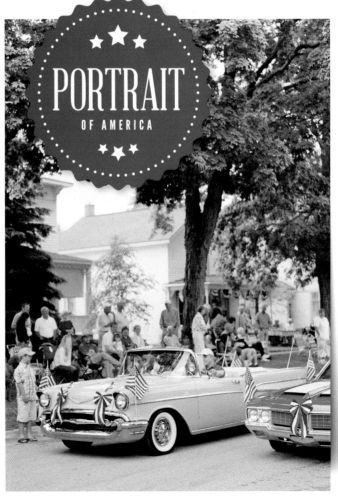

FOURTH OF JULY PARADE

Frankfort, Michigan

Old-fashioned patriotism's still alive and well at small-town independence day celebrations across the nation.

What ►► The laid-back parade in this town boasts classic cars, colorful floats, a high school marching band, and kids riding bikes decked out in red, white, and blue streamers.

When ►► For more than 100 years, when July 4 rolls around, nearly every citizen in this tiny village on the shores of Lake Michigan (pop. 1,513) participates in the event—or cheers from the sidelines.

Why ►► "Our parade's not flashy or high-tech," says native son Joshua Mills, the city superintendent. "It's just a lot of fun—and a great way to show off community spirit."

PORTRAIT
OF AMERICA

FABULOUS FINGER FOOD

▲◄ **Start things off with deviled eggs.** Keep it simple or kick it up a notch with caramelized onions, cilantro, or curry powder.

◄ **Then move on to barbecued kebabs.** Pineapple, peppers, mushroom, ham: anything goes—so long as it can be slid onto a skewer.

◄◄ **Finish strong with ice cream sandwiches.** Nothing beats the richness or portability of these treats, which pair store-bought cookies and ice cream. Even better? You can prepare these babies in advance.

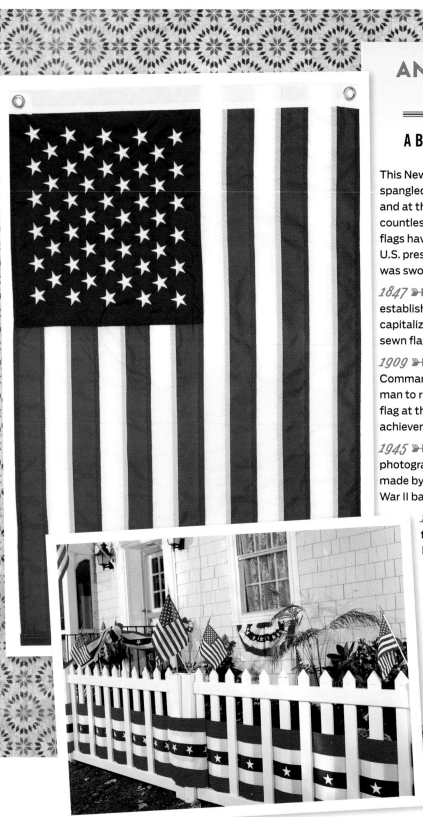

ANNIN FLAGMAKERS

Roseland, New Jersey

A Brief History of Annin Flagmakers

This New Jersey—based company creates the star-spangled banners that hang in the White House and at the United Nations—not to mention from countless front porches across America. Annin flags have also flown at the inauguration of every U.S. president since 1849, when Zachary Taylor was sworn into office.

1847 ➤➤ Brothers Benjamin and Edward Annin establish Annin Flagmakers in New York City to capitalize on their father's success making hand-sewn flags for ships on Manhattan's waterfront.

1909 ➤➤ After an arduous nine-month trek, Commander Robert E. Peary becomes the first man to reach the North Pole. He stakes an Annin flag at the top of the world to commemorate the achievement.

1945 ➤➤ Joe Rosenthal's Pulitzer Prize—winning photograph shows soldiers erecting a U.S. flag made by Annin on Iwo Jima during the pivotal World War II battle in Japan.

1969 ➤➤ Astronaut Buzz Aldrin poses next to Old Glory during NASA's Apollo 11 lunar landing. A horizontal rod along the top of the Annin flag ensures it "waves" despite the moon's zero gravity.

2014 ➤➤ Now a sixth-generation family business, Annin Flagmakers sells about five million American flags a year.

PORTRAIT
OF AMERICA

◀ **Don't shy away from red, white, and blue.** Today's the day to let your All-American flag fly, so put out napkins, ribbons, and fabric scraps in Old Glory colors to work decorating the buffet.

PORTRAIT
OF AMERICA

THE TERVIS TUMBLER CO.

North Venice, Florida

Florida's Tervis Tumbler Co. cups have kept drinks cool for 65 years.

Back in 1946, Detroit engineers Frank Cotter and George Howlett Davis hit upon a refreshing idea: an insulated plastic cup with double walls that maintain a beverage's temperature and provide a spot for displaying fun fabric designs. Cotter and Davis dubbed their venture Tervis, a combination of their last names, and it wasn't long before area shops began carrying the duo's creation. Now based on Florida's west coast, Tervis offers five tumbler sizes, plus mugs and ice buckets, all made-to-order.

1955 ⇉ Cotter and Davis patent their drinking-glass concept and soon sell the business to Florida entrepreneur John C. Winslow.

1984 ⇉ Tervis moves beyond nautical and golf themes with more girlish motifs, such as colorful confetti. Twenty-seven years later, the factory turns out more than 1,000 options, from customized monograms to barnyard images.

1995 ⇉ The company adds licensed tumblers for a client list that grows to include the Kentucky Derby, Coca-Cola, and the NFL.

2011 ⇉ Tervis expands its headquarters, increasing production capacity by 50 percent—to 90,000 cups per day.

The New Rules HOLIDAYS

Then ⇥ Holidays are formal, sit-down affairs that require hours of prep, ironing napkins, and polishing silverware.

Now ⇥ Joyous potlucks are fun for all—including the host!

Then ⇥ Decades of dry Thanksgiving turkeys spark the catchphrase, "Should've bought a Butterball!"

Now ⇥ Whether deep-fried, roasted in bourbon, or brined overnight, the latest twists on turkey preparations make for seriously succulent birds.

Then ⇥ Fireworks were sparklers and bottle rockets.

Now ⇥ Fourth of July shows have gotten a whole lot more spectacular. Professional pyrotechnics are regularly accompanied by music from live orchestras or pop hits synced up with the crackling blasts of light.

◄ **Give drinks extra flourish.** Turn paper doilies, card stock, and wooden skewers into pretty parasols with major punch.

▲ **Last grasp** Skeletal stencils
(at countryliving.com/halloween)
make these carvings look as if they're
reaching out from beyond the grave.

▲ **Great balls of fire** Set your hearth ablaze with these rip-roaring flames from countryliving.com/halloween.

▲ **Out on a limb** A sturdy bookcase provides the structure needed for this painted-tree idea to take root.

three INSPIRED *sweet treats*

◄ **Turn a Granny Smith into a s'more.** Outshine the usual candy apple by dipping yours in marshmallows, chocolate, and graham cracker crumbs.

▼ **Weave your own tangled web.** The secret to this elegantly eerie dessert is melted marshmallows.

► **Give a frosted sheet cake grave intentions.** The tombstones are fashioned from Pepperidge Farm's Milano and Bordeaux cookies, while crushed chocolate wafers in front conjure dirt mounds.

▲ **Phantom presence** Keep up ghostly appearances with this witty reflection, made with frosted window film.

◄ **Spell it out.** As a smart alternative to pumpkin carving, this Vermont family sends their message with paint.

◀ **Turn over a new leaf.** Hit the road, jack! This naturally brilliant idea pairs colorful leaves decoupaged on white gourds.

▼ **Spread your wings.** The secret to these moth-adorned marvels? Weather-resistant vinyl decals.

▶ **Pride of place** Let revelers know they're at the right address by emblazoning your house number—and hometown—on pumpkins with number stickers and a decal of your state.

◄ **Give your bird a leg up.**
The secret to this decidedly tender turkey? Roasting it in a pan of bourbon!

► **Ripe fruit is as lush as any floral centerpiece.**
Ruby red pomegranates plus inexpensive foliage yield major drama with minimal effort.

★★ *Five* ★★
REASONS TO LOVE
owning an
HISTORIC INN OR TAVERN

1 You may not ever get to peek into the Lincoln bedroom, but the country is dotted with places where George Washington slept—and you can sleep there, too.

2 Who among us doesn't fantasize about running a bed-and-breakfast?

3 These places enjoy the old-fashioned elegance of scale: big reception areas and lots of bedrooms.

4 This is where you find the really wide-plank floors.

5 It's not all hard cider and darts, either: Phi Beta Kappa, the nation's oldest academic honor society, was founded in Virginia's Raleigh's Tavern in 1776.

PORTRAIT
OF AMERICA

NORDIC WARE
Minneapolis, Minnesota

The dish on Minnesota's Nordic Ware—inventors of the iconic Bundt pan.

Despite a name that sounds Scandinavian, Nordic Ware's history is as American as apple pie. In 1946, Minneapolis engineer H. David Dalquist and his wife, Dotty, started designing bakeware to sell locally. Four years later, they introduced their most famous creation: the Bundt pan. Today, the company—run by the couple's son, David—offers more than 350 products from skillets to grill tools.

1950 ⇒ Dalquist models his Bundt pan on an old German design and trademarks the name, based on the German word for a gathering.

1966 ⇒ Ella Rita Helfrich of Houston uses a Bundt pan for her winning Tunnel of Fudge cake recipe at the Pillsbury Bake-Off.

1980 ⇒ Nordic Ware debuts a new invention, the Micro-Go-Round—the rotating plate used in microwave ovens.

2009 ⇒ The brand adds some 60,000 square feet to its Minneapolis factory, where it now manufactures 50 variations on the classic Bundt pan.

◄ **Practical and precious pie birds** Baked in a pastry, these ceramic utensils offer an adorable way to let off steam. And displayed on kitchen shelves, they positively sing.

▼ **Build a better pie.** Use ice-cold butter and water to yield a flaky piecrust—and chill txhe dough before rolling.

▲ **Help chairs take flight.** Even the seats in this Illinois dining room get into the holiday spirit with angel wings.

▶ **Tablescapes don't have to be a ton of work.** In Washington state, this charming woodland scene requires little more than loose sprigs of greenery in sap buckets, toy deer, and bottlebrush trees—all unified by a linen runner.

TUCKAMONY FARM

New Hope, Pennsylvania

This Christmas tree farm continues the cut-your-own tradition in Pennsylvania.

When ⇾ Starting the Friday after Thanksgiving and continuing through Christmas Eve, folks venture out to this 72-acre spread to find, and fell, their ideal evergreens from among eight different species, including blue spruces and Scots pines.

Who ⇾ Malcolm Crooks (below, with his grandson Lars) expanded his father's business by more than tripling the amount of planted land. Today, Lars runs the operation. "It's amazing to see 75-foot-tall Norway spruces and realize that my great-grandfather planted them," he says.

Why ⇾ "You can go to a big-box store and buy a tree for about $25," explains Lars, who charges $59, "but people come here for the experience." (tuckamony.com)

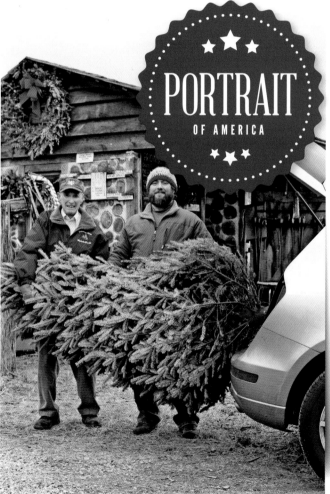

PORTRAIT
OF AMERICA

▲ **Discover a whole world of nifty nutcrackers.** Venture beyond the classic Christmas soldier and you'll find an army of other adorable styles worth shelling out for.

◄ **Give snow globes a farmhouse makeover.**
Mason jars recast these tiny holiday wonderlands in a whole new American light.

▶ **Spread cheer in unexpected ways.** Easy-to-overlook bookcases get a graphic jolt from plaid giftwrap in this Washington–state home.

▼ **Make your tree come alive.** Turn poinsettias into living ornaments in a flash with floral water tubes.

▶▶ **Arrange branches in a vase for an easy tabletop "tree."** This beauty is adorned with chandelier prisms and gold-painted walnuts.

Trim Your Tree in a Jiffy

These sweet and simple items are ready to hang:

★ Pinecones

★ Silhouette gift tags

★ Candy canes

★ Ribbons—as garlands or tied on in bows

PHOTO CREDITS

Cover (from left to right): Gridley & Graves, Lara Robby/Studio D, John Gruen
Alamy: David Ridley: 73; H. Mark Weidman Photography: 136; Andreas von Einsiedel: 60 (left); Tom Zuback: 91; Corbis: Jaak Nilson: 164 (bottom); Getty Images: Bloomberg: 29 (bottom); Chris Clor: 35 (bottom); Carl Dahlstedt: 49 (top); Daly and Newton: 85 (bottom right) Emma Farrer: 83 (bottom right) Chris Gramly: 65 (bottom right); Melanie Acevedo: 66; Lucas Allen: 17, 26 (right), 32–33, 60 (right), 90, 94, 99, 111 (bottom), 114 (right), 116 (left), 122 (top), 134, 172 (bottom), 173; Cedric Angeles: 120; Courtesy of Annin Flagmakers, Roseland, NJ: 152 (bottom); Matt Armendariz: 158 (left); Authentique Paper, LLC, "Dignity" (background): 14, 29, 39, 95, 103, 12, 126, 141, 152, 154, 166; Burcu Avsar: 14, 40, 162 (bottom), 163; Quentin Bacon: 48, 56, 105, 145 (bottom), 150 (top left); Christopher Baker: 8, 53, 79 (right); Stacey Brandford: 117 (left); Langdon Clay: 95; Colin Cooke: 138 (left), 139 (right); Roger Davies: 97, 101, 130–131 (right); Trevor Dixon: 169 (right); Miki Duisterhof: 12–13 (right), 21 (right), 29 (top), 39, 47 (2), 96, 103, 111 (top), 123, 145 (top), 165; Philip Ficks: 50, 69; Don Freeman: 28 (left), 138 (right), 139 (left); Philip Friedman/Studio D: 20, 146 (left), 164 (top); Dana Gallagher: 34, 35 (left), 76, 160; Alison Gootee/Studio D: 11, 25 (left), 73 (left), 118 (right), 162 (top); Gridley & Graves: 41 (2), 74–75 (left); John Gruen: 4, 54 (left), 137, 148; Audrey Hall: 144; Alec Hemer: 27, 28 (right), 72, 83 (left), 98, 106, 110; Aimee Herring: 10, 18 , 82, 104, 122 (bottom); Karl Juengel / Studio D: 152; Ray Kachatorian: 150 (bottom left); Keller and Keller: 141; John Kernick: 20–21 (center), 156–157 (3), 158 (right), 161; Max Kim-Bee: 16, 22, 23, 24, 25 (right), 31, 59, 62–63, 64–65 (center), 67, 78, 85 (left), 107 (left), 112, 124, 133 (bottom), 146 (right); Mark Lohman: 46, 61, 132; Kate Mathis: 77 (right), 126, 133 (top), 166; Ericka McConnell: 154; James Merrell: 49 (bottom), 55 (right); Laura Moss: 6, 64 (left), 100, 102, 168 (left); J Muckle /Studio D: 80; Dan Nelken: 51 (right); Marcus Nilsson: 167 (right); Helen Norman: 12; Kana Okada: 150–151 (center), 153, 166, 167 (left); Victoria Pearson: 30, 44, 58, 68, 88–89, 92, 119, 125, 127, 130 (left), 142–143 (right), 155, 168–169 (center), 172 (top); Lara Robby/Studio D: 26 (left), 50–51 (center), 114 (left), 128, 142, 171; Lisa Romerein: 70, 108–109; Hector Sanchez: 159; Anson Smart: 38; Buff Strickland: 151 (right); Annie Tritt: 129 (right); Jonny Valiant: 118 (left), 147; William Waldron: 43, 55 (right), 75 (right), 88 (left), 117 (right), 128–129 (center); Bjorn Wallander: 3, 15, 19, 36, 42, 45, 52 (left), 71, 79 (right), 84, 86, 93, 107 (right), 113, 115, 135; Anna Williams: 170; Andrea Wyner: 81, 140

INDEX

AVON PUBLIC LIBRARY
BOX 977 / 200 BENCHMARK RD.
AVON, COLORADO 81620